What Is

The
Apostles' Creed

Learning About The Apostles' Creed

What Is the Apostles' Creed?

Written by G. L. Reed
Art by Megan Jeffery

Joan Walker . . . . . *Editor*
LeeDell B. Stickler . . . . . *Senior Editor*
Charlotte Dawson Overlay . . . . . *Production Editor*
Arvis Guilbault . . . . . *Designer*

Credits:
p. 4: The Apostles' Creed, Traditional Version (The United Methodisty Hymnal, No. 881)
p. 28: A Modern Affirmation (The United Methodist Hymnal, No. 885)

ISBN 978-0-687-49317-3

PACP00312540-07

12 13 14 15 16- 10 9 8 7

Manufactured in the United States of America

CONTENTS

The Apostles' Creed, Traditional Version 4

What Is? 5

The Code 6

A Creed. 7

The Apostles' Creed 8

What Do You Believe? 9

Filling in The Blanks 10

I Believe 11

Learning the Words 12

Telling the Story 13

Mother Mary 14

Who Was Pontius Pilate? . . 15

The Final Days 16

I Believe 17

Connecting the Words. 18

Breaking It Down 19

I Believe 20

Finding the Words. 21

Putting It in Order 22

Finding the Words. 23

Taking a Moment 24

Trivia Test 25-26

What I Believe. 27

A Different Affirmation of Faith 28

Write Your Own Creed 29

Answers. 30-31

Activities You Can Do at Home 32

THE APOSTLES' CREED

(Traditional Version)

I believe in God the Father Almighty,
   maker of heaven and earth;

And in Jesus Christ his only Son our Lord:
   who was conceived by the Holy Spirit,
      born of the Virgin Mary,
      suffered under Pontius Pilate,
      was crucified, dead, and buried;*
   the third day he rose from the dead;
   he ascended into heaven,
      and sitteth at the right hand of God the Father
   Almighty; from thence he shall come to judge the
   quick and the dead.

I believe in the Holy Spirit,
   the holy catholic** church,
   the communion of saints,
   the forgiveness of sins,
   the resurrection of the body,
   and the life everlasting. Amen.

*Traditional use of this creed sometimes includes these words: "He descended into hell."
**universal

4

WHAT IS??

So what is the Apostles' Creed? We repeat it in unison during worship at church. We call it an "affirmation of faith." In the Apostles' Creed, we are stating what we as Christians believe.

This book will help you learn something about the traditional Apostles' Creed. It's also a good way to help you memorize the creed so you that you can say it during worship from the heart.

Along the way you will have to find a few clues and finish a few puzzles. There are also some hidden words to search for and codes to break. When you are done, if someone asks you, "As a Christian, what do you believe?" you can answer them.

If you need some help with the activities, the answers are in the back of the book. You will also find some extra projects there you can do by yourself or with friends. Have fun!

The Code

A creed is a statement of belief. We, as Christians, have certain beliefs. We state these beliefs in the form of a written or spoken creed. Each word of the Apostles' Creed tells us what we believe— about God, about Jesus, about the Holy Spirit, about the church.

Use the code to fill in the blanks for the words on the next page. Learn more about what a creed is and how a creed can influence your life.

1 = A	14 = N
2 = B	15 = O
3 = C	16 = P
4 = D	17 = Q
5 = E	18 = R
6 = F	19 = S
7 = G	20 = T
8 = H	21 = U
9 = I	22 = V
10 = J	23 = W
11 = K	24 = X
12 = L	25 = Y
13 = M	26 = Z

(Answers on page 30)

A CREED

"
13 5 1 14 19   9   2 5 12 9 5 22 5 "

___ ___ ___ ___ ___ ___ ___ .
9 14   12 1 20 9 14

___ ___ ___ ___ ___ ___ ___ ___ ___
20 5 12 12 19   23 8 1 20

___ ___ ___ ___ ___ ___ ___
19 15 13 5 15 14 5

___ ___ ___ ___ ___ ___ ___ ___ .
2 5 12 9 5 22 5 19

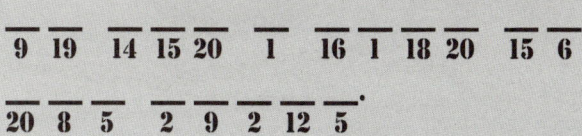

___ ___ ___ ___ ___ ___ ___ ___ ___ ___ ___ ___
9 19   14 15 20   1   16 1 18 20 15 6

___ ___ ___ ___ ___ ___ ___ .
20 8 5   2 9 2 12 5

___ ___ ___ ___ ___   ___ ___ ___ ___ ___ ___ ___ .
1 12 9 6 5   4 5 3 9 19 9 15 14

THE APOSTLES' CREED

Read the statements below. Four of them are true. Find the statement that is not true. Check all of the true statements. Put an **X** on the false one.

☐ Legend says that the apostles wrote this creed ten days after the ascension of Jesus (but it's only a legend).

☐ The Apostles' Creed has been around for over 1000 years.

☐ The Apostles' Creed is a part of the Bible.

☐ The Apostles' Creed is one of the oldest creeds of our Christian faith.

☐ The Apostles' Creed was used to instruct candidates for baptism in the early church.

8

(Answers on page 30)

What Do You Believe?

In the circles below are the words to the beginning of The Apostles' Creed. Start with "I Believe" and connect the words in order by drawing a line from one word to the next. Then write the first phrase of the Apostles' Creed in the space provided at the bottom of the page.

I believe

God

Father

the

Almighty

in

(Answers on page 30)

Filling in The Blanks

What does the Apostle's Creed say that we believe about God? Fill in the missing letters below to complete the words about what we, as Christians, believe about God. Use the letters at the bottom of the page in the blank spaces.

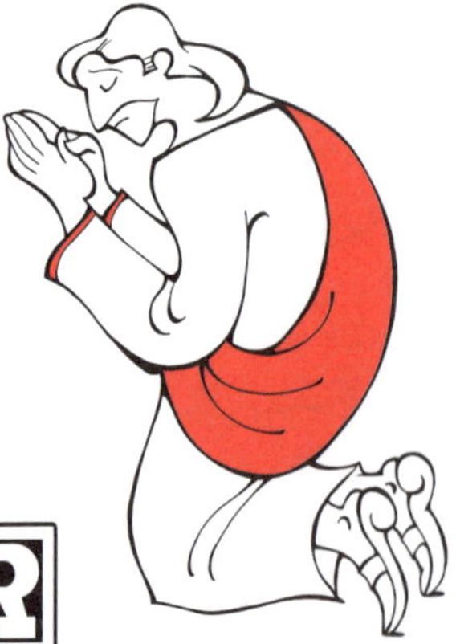

K
N
T
O
E
M
R
H
D

☐ A ☐ E R
☐ F ☐ E A V ☐
A N ☐ ☐ E A ☐ ☐ H

(Answers on page 30)

10

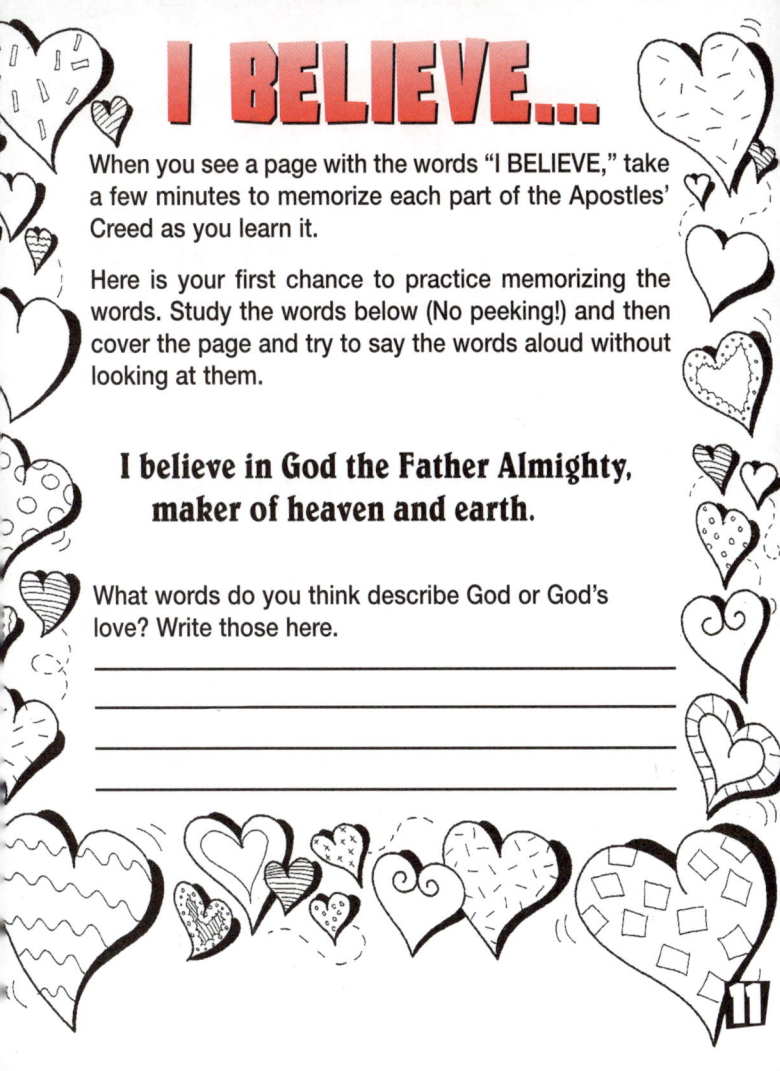

I BELIEVE...

When you see a page with the words "I BELIEVE," take a few minutes to memorize each part of the Apostles' Creed as you learn it.

Here is your first chance to practice memorizing the words. Study the words below (No peeking!) and then cover the page and try to say the words aloud without looking at them.

I believe in God the Father Almighty, maker of heaven and earth.

What words do you think describe God or God's love? Write those here.

_____

_____

_____

_____

Learning the Words

Unscramble these letters to find the words from the next part of the Apostles' Creed.

A Clue: a special person from the Bible
SUJES HCRSIT

— — — — —   — — — — — —

A Clue: not daughter, but a
NSO

— — —

A Clue: another name for Jesus
ROLD

— — — —

Now use the words above to complete this part of the creed.

And in __ __ __ __ __
__ __ __ __ __ __ **his only**
__ __ __ **our** __ __ __ __.

(Answers on page 30)

Telling the Story

What do we, as Christians, believe about Jesus? The statements we say in this part of the Apostles' Creed also tell us some of the story of the life of Jesus.

Find the words to the part of the Apostles' Creed (See p. 4) that tells of the birth of Jesus. Fill in the boxes with the words you find. Then fill in the blanks below.

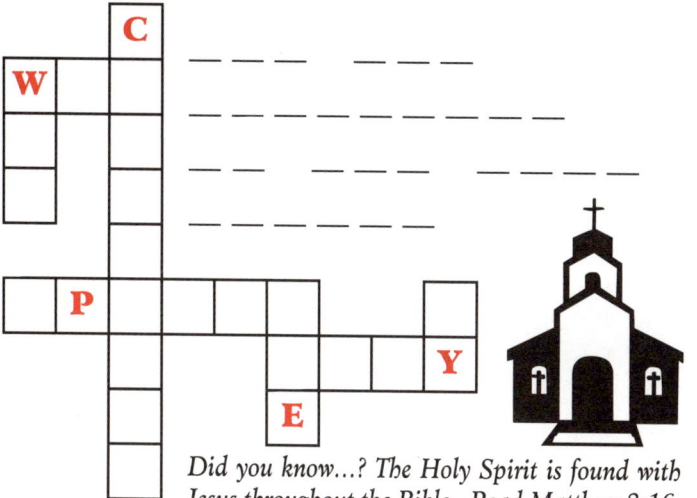

Did you know…? The Holy Spirit is found with Jesus throughout the Bible. Read Matthew 3:16.

(Answers on page 30)

13

MOTHER MARY

The next statement from the Apostles' Creed tells us about Jesus' mother. Find the letters in connecting boxes and write the words of the statement below.

Hint: starts with the letter **B** and ends with the letter **Y**.

A	**B**	L	M	K	R	S
N	O	M	C	Y	X	E
G	R	I	K	O	V	E
U	N	O	F	T	L	C
Y	S	A	N	H	D	I
G	R	I	V	E	S	A
I	N	M	A	R	**Y**	Z

B_ _ _ _   _ _   _ _ _ _

_ _ _ _ _ _   _ _ _ **Y**

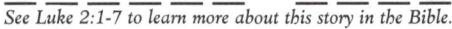

See Luke 2:1-7 to learn more about this story in the Bible.

(Answers on page 30)

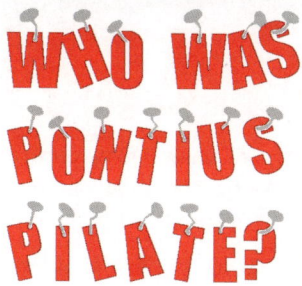

WHO WAS PONTIUS PILATE?

Towards the end of Jesus' ministry, he was arrested and sent to the Roman governor of Judea, whose name was Pontius Pilate. There Jesus was questioned, beaten and then turned over to the Jewish religious council to be crucified.

Here is the next part of the Apostles' Creed. Unscramble the words below and learn more about this story.

_ _ _ _ _ _ _ _   **UFFSREDE**

_ _ _ _ _   **DNURE**

_ _ _ _ _ _   **ONPIUST**

_ _ _ _ _ _   **PIATLE**

Think about it... The Apostles' Creed is not a part of the Bible, but it does tell us about stories from the Bible. When we read the Bible, we can learn more about Jesus, God, and the Holy Spirit. How can the Bible help you understand your faith?

See Matthew 27:1-2, 11-14, 24-26 to learn more about this story in the Bible.
(Answers on page 30)

THE FINAL DAYS

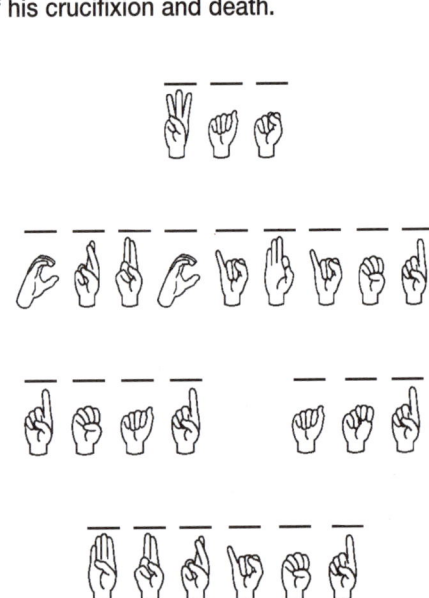

A N
B O
C P
D Q
E R
F S
G T
H U
I V
J W
K X
L Y
M Z

The Bible tells of the last days of Jesus' life on earth and his ascension into heaven. We hear these stories during the Easter season and also in the next part of the creed.

Break the code and write the words in the spaces below. Think about what you have learned about Jesus and the time of his crucifixion and death.

See Matthew 27:32-61, Luke 23:26-56 to learn more about this story in the Bible.

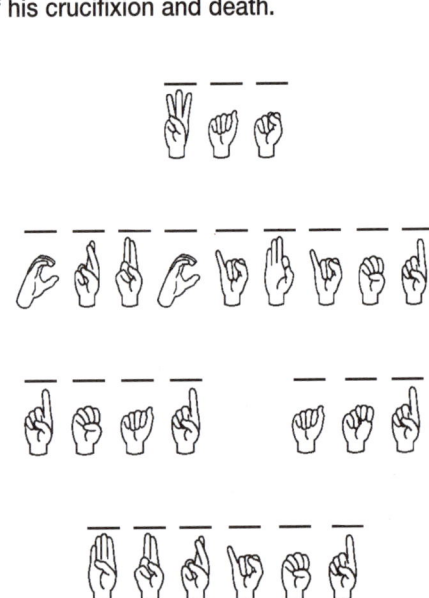

16

(Answers on page 30)

I BELIEVE...

Here is another chance to practice memorizing the words. Study the words below (No peeking!) and then cover the page and try to say the words aloud without looking at them.

I believe in God the Father Almighty,
   maker of heaven and earth;

And in Jesus Christ his only Son our Lord:
   who was conceived by the Holy Spirit,
      born of the Virgin Mary,
      suffered under Pontius Pilate,
      was crucified, dead, and buried;

What words can you use to describe what Jesus taught us to do and be? Write those here.

_____

_____

_____

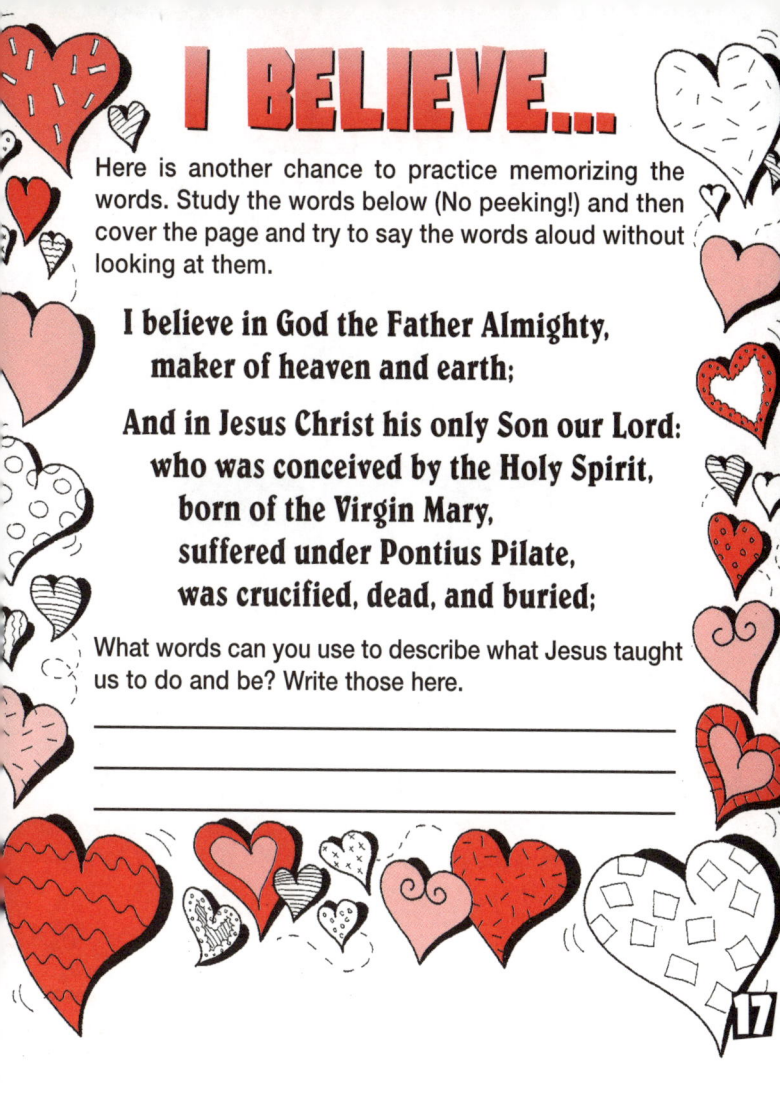

Connecting the Words

Draw a line to connect the boxes that hold the words for the next part of the creed. Once all the boxes are connected, move from box to box to read this part aloud.

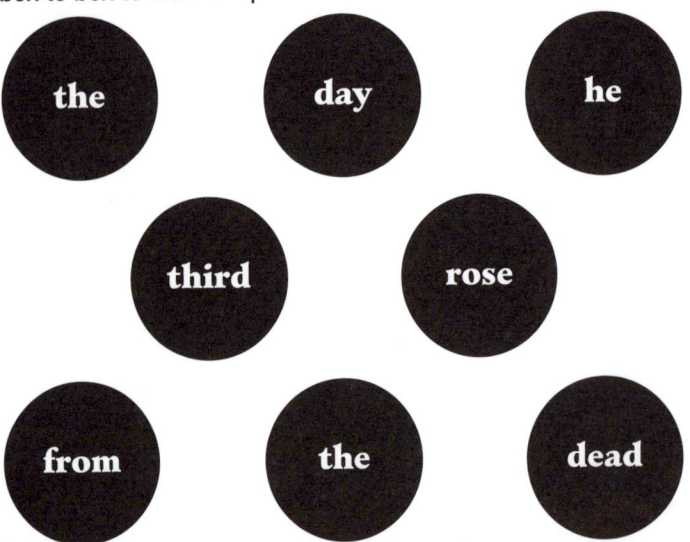

the **day** **he**

third **rose**

from **the** **dead**

Think about it... When Jesus rose from the dead, he returned to talk with Mary and the disciples. Jesus also promised to leave us with a helper. How does Jesus continue to be with each of us today?

See Matthew 27:62-28:1-20, Mark 16:1-8 to learn more about this story in the Bible.

(Answers on page 30)

Breaking it Down

Separate the letters below to find words that tell you the next statement about Jesus from the Apostles' Creed.

Hint: start from the center of the spiral and work your way out.

The spiral reads: HE ASCENDED INTO HEAVEN, AND SITTETH ON THE RIGHT HAND OF GOD THE FATHER ALMIGHTY. FROM THENCE HE SHALL COME TO JUDGE THE QUICK AND THE DEAD.

**Quick in this case means "living."

(Answers on page 31)

19

I BELIEVE...

Take another minute to practice memorizing the creed. Study the words below and then cover the page (No peeking!) and try to say them aloud.

I believe in God the Father Almighty,
   maker of heaven and earth;

And in Jesus Christ his only Son our Lord:
   who was conceived by the Holy Spirit,
      born of the Virgin Mary,
      suffered under Pontius Pilate,
      was crucified, dead, and buried;
   the third day he rose from the dead;
   he ascended into heaven,
      and sitteth at the right hand of God the Father Almighty; from thence he shall come to judge the quick and the dead.

As Christians, we believe that one day Jesus will return to the earth. What are some of the things we will be judged on when Jesus returns?

_____

_____

Finding the Words

Another thing Christians believe is that God sent the Holy Spirit to be our helper and guide. Jesus taught us how to live. The Holy Spirit is a personal guide given to us by God. The Holy Spirit is God's voice inside of us. It helps us make decisions and helps us know we are doing things as Jesus would.

Circle the words that complete a statement about our belief in this special gift. Write the phrase below.

— _ _ _ _ _ _ _

_ _ _ _ _ _ _ _ _ _

_ _ _ _ _ _

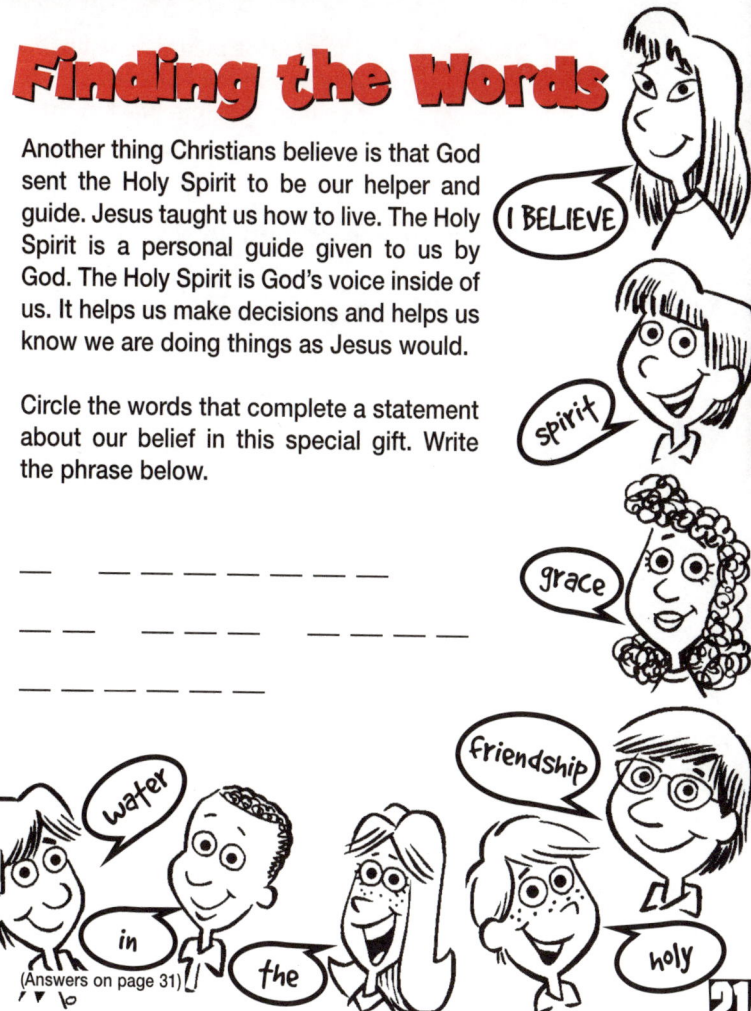

(Answers on page 31)

Putting It in Order

The phrases below make up the final part of the Apostles' Creed. See if you can put them in order.

Number each phrase 1 through 6.

___ the resurrection of the body,

___ the forgiveness of sins,

___ the holy catholic church,

___ Amen.

___ and the life everlasting.

___ the communion of saints,

What does Amen mean?

_____

_____

(Answers on page 31)

FINDING THE WORDS

Find words from the Apostles' Creed in the puzzle. The words you are looking for are listed beside the puzzle. When you finish, say The Apostles' Creed from memory.

The Apostles' Creed

ALMIGHTY
BELIEVE
CHRIST
CHURCH
CRUCIFIED
DEAD
EARTH
HEAVEN
HOLY
LORD
PILATE
QUICK
SAINTS
SPIRIT
SUFFERED
THIRD

(Answers on page 31)

Taking a Moment

Try to fill in the blanks below from memory. Then look back at page 4 to check your answers.

I _ _ _ _ _ _ _ _ in _ _ _ the Father _ _ _ _ _ _ _ _ _, maker of _ _ _ _ _ _ _ _ and _ _ _ _ _ _;
And in _ _ _ _ _ _ _ _ _ _ _ _ _ _ his only son our _ _ _ _ _: who was conceived by the _ _ _ _ _ _ _ _ _ _ _ _,
born of the Virgin _ _ _ _ _, suffered under Pontius _ _ _ _ _ _ _, was crucified, dead, and buried; the _ _ _ _ _ _ day he rose from the dead; he _ _ _ _ _ _ _ _ _ into heaven, and sitteth at the right hand of _ _ _ the Father _ _ _ _ _ _ _ _ _ _; from thence he shall come to judge the quick and the dead. I _ _ _ _ _ _ _ _ _ in the _ _ _ _ _ _ _ _ _ _ _ _ _, the holy catholic church, the communion of saints, the forgiveness of _ _ _ _ _, the resurrection of the body, and the _ _ _ _ _ everlasting _ _ _ _.

24

Creed means:

1. blessings.
2. I believe.
3. I am faithful.

We say the Apostles' Creed:

1. to fill time in church.
2. to remember the apostles from the Bible.
3. to make a statement of what we believe.

The Apostles' Creed has been around for:

1. about 100 years.
2. about 500 years.
3. over 1000 years.

(Answers on page 31)

The Apostles' Creed tells us something about:

1. our Christian faith.

2. the apostles.

3. how to treat each other.

The Apostles' Creed was used as

1. a test for people who wanted to be disciples.

2. a secret password to the early church houses.

3. instruction for persons who were to be baptized.

The Apostles' Creed can be found

1. in the Book of Matthew.

2. in the Book of Luke.

3. in the Book of John.

4. in the hymnal.

(Answers on page 31)

What I Believe

When you say the words to a creed, you are saying something about what you believe. You are also saying something about the life you are choosing to lead.

God has a plan for you. In the Christian faith, Jesus set the example of how we can live our lives. The Holy Spirit is our guide, helping us to know right from wrong. Check the statements that match what you believe.

_____ When I pray, I can find comfort and guidance.

_____ Jesus shows us actions we can take in our lives.

_____ When I need to make a decision, I can pray with the Holy Spirit.

_____ I am forgiven of my sins and allowed a chance to try again.

_____ Life with Jesus offers God's love to all people.

_____ God is the creator of all things.

A DIFFERENT AFFIRMATION

We believe in God the Father,
  infinite in wisdom, power, and love,
  whose mercy is over all his works,
  and whose will is ever directed to his children's good.

We believe in Jesus Christ,
  Son of God and Son of man,
  the gift of the Father's unfailing grace,
  the ground of our hope,
  and the promise of our deliverance from sin and death.

We believe in the Holy Spirit
  as the divine presence in our lives,
  whereby we are kept in perpetual remembrance
  of the truth of Christ,
  and find strength and help in time of need.

We believe that this faith should manifest itself
  in the service of love
  as set forth in the example of our blessed Lord,
  to the end
  that the kingdom of God may come upon the earth.

    Amen.